Navy SEALs Mental Toughness

A Guide To Developing An Unbeatable Mind

© 2016 Chris Lambertsen. All Rights Reserved.

Table of Contents

Preface 5

Navy SEAL Training 7

BUD/S and Hell Week 15

Earn Your Trident Every Day 25

SEAL Missions 34

Mental Toughness 56

Understanding Fear 67

Conquering Fear 73

Pursuit of Excellence 91

Becoming Mentally Tough 95

The Meaning of Success 105

Preface

In my many years of experience studying high achievers, I have found that many of the same qualities that are essential to succeed as a Navy SEAL are the same qualities required for success in any endeavor.

This book will introduce to you many of the methods used by this elite force to develop mental toughness and self-confidence in their warriors. These techniques also apply to anyone who is interested in becoming more mentally tough, and who is willing to work toward achieving their specific personal and professional goals.

Learning about how Navy SEALs approach situations and the mentality with which they function, will enable you to contrast your outlook and mindset when faced with challenges or obstacles.

By reading this book you are already a step closer to success. Learn from these men and then adhere to their methodology, and I can guarantee positive results on your journey toward your goals.

Navy SEAL Training

The road to becoming a Navy SEAL is long and hard. Following is a short summary of the stages that make up the Navy SEAL selection and training courses that every SEAL must go through in order to become a member of this elite force.

STAGE 1: Naval Special Warfare Prep School
(8 Weeks – Great Lakes, Illinois)

For the majority of prospective SEALs, the journey to becoming a member of the Teams begins after the completion of basic training (boot camp) and assignment to Prep School. This course averages eight weeks in duration, and is supervised by active-duty SEALs and other Naval Special Warfare personnel. In this course, there is a heavy emphasis on physical conditioning. The goal is to condition students to the point where they meet or exceed the established standards for admission to BUD/S, and also to ensure their bodies are toughened to the degree necessary to survive the rigors of the subsequent BUD/S orientation course and BUD/S First Phase.

STAGE 2: BUD/S Orientation Course
(3 Weeks – Coronado, California)

During this course students become familiarized with the Naval Special Warfare Training Center at Coronado and get their first real taste of the daily routine associated with being a BUD/S student. Physical training (PT) remains a top priority, and the intensity of the PT sessions means they train at a much higher level. The students are taught how to make their way, properly and safely, through the legendary BUD/S obstacle course. They also receive basic instruction on some of the equipment that they utilize in First Phase. The students remain in Coronado until they graduate from BUD/S or are dropped from the training program.

STAGE 3: BUD/S First Phase – Basic Conditioning
(7 Weeks)

The primary mission of First Phase is to eliminate the students who lack the will or the physical ability to successfully complete BUD/S. This filtering process is achieved by continuous, rigorous physical-training sessions and other training evolutions. These evolutions are all associated with various training and educational goals, but the reality is that everything about First Phase is designed to push the students to the edge of their perceived physical and mental limitations. As you might expect, First Phase has the highest attrition rate for BUD/S classes—historically around 75 percent.

During this phase the standards and scores required to pass various evolutions and graded events are elevated at the beginning of each week, making each week of First Phase tougher than the previous one. In addition to physical training, students are exposed to various water-related training evolutions, both in the Pacific Ocean and in the BUD/S training pool. A great deal of emphasis is placed on development of a team mentality and teamwork among the students. The class is broken down into boat teams consisting of six to eight students, and almost every training evolution is conducted as a competition, pitting one boat team against the others, and the losers pay a high price.

The fourth week of this phase is devoted to the infamous and much-feared Hell Week, which is a 5½-day evolution consisting of nonstop physical training and other activities designed to make the students colder and more exhausted than they have ever been. This is, of course, intended to make each student continually reflect upon just how badly he wants to be a Navy SEAL. For many, the rigors of Hell Week are simply more than they can endure, and throughout the week, it is quite common to hear the brass bell being rung three times as yet another student quits the course. Hell Week will be covered in greater detail in the next chapter, since it is such an important factor in the development of the mental toughness that's associated with Navy SEALs.

STAGE 4: BUD/S Second Phase – Combat Diving
(7 Weeks)

During this phase students are trained as basic combat swimmers. Successful Second Phase candidates demonstrate a high level of comfort in the water and the ability to perform in stressful, and often uncomfortable, situations. Candidates who are not completely comfortable in the water often struggle to complete this phase.

As you might expect, students spend the majority of their time in the water learning and practicing various surface and underwater skills. Throughout this phase the students will be evaluated regarding their competence and confidence while in the water—both attributes are absolute necessities for a Navy SEAL.

The students are introduced to open- and closed-circuit diving. Both techniques are commonly used in operational units. There is a significant amount of classroom instruction associated with learning both types of diving, making this phase as academically challenging as it is physically challenging. In addition to training to become a combat swimmer, the students are continually challenged by various graded physical-training evolutions, such as timed distance runs, open ocean swims, and, of course, the ever-present obstacle course.

STAGE 5: BUD/S Third Phase – Land Warfare Training
(7 Weeks)

During this phase the students get their first real exposure to the many tools and techniques that are related to their chosen profession or specialty. They receive instruction on a variety of small arms, and they spend quite a bit of time becoming proficient in their use. Also covered in great detail is the employment of various types of explosives, land navigation, patrolling, rappelling, marksmanship, and small-unit tactics.

Most of the classroom instruction associated with this phase takes place at the BUD/S training compound. The last few weeks of the phase are spent on San Clemente Island, where the Navy maintains live-fire ranges and demolition ranges. Students run through a series of graded evolutions and practical-application exercises during their time on the island.

Throughout this phase the emphasis on physical training remains high and, as always, standards and passing scores for timed runs, swims, and the obstacle course are progressively elevated to ensure that the students find each subsequent week more demanding than the previous one. This continues until the class reaches the long-awaited BUD/S graduation ceremony.

STAGE 6: SEAL Qualification Training
(26 Weeks – Various Locations)

Once the students have successfully completed BUD/S, they attend a course known as SEAL Qualification Training (SQT). This training is designed to transition the students from basically-trained combat swimmers and warriors to highly-trained special operators. They must become proficient in many individual and team-based skills, which are essential if they are to operate successfully as a fully qualified SEAL. In essence, this training is very much a "finishing school" that is intended to produce graduates who can be assigned to an operational unit. The goal is to produce SEALs who are immediately capable of performing alongside more seasoned and more experienced teammates.

Students undergo advanced weapons training and extensive instruction in small-unit tactics, they are exposed to advanced demolitions techniques, and become more proficient at land navigation during both day and night operations.

Parachute operations—both static line and free fall—are also in the curriculum. The students receive the official designation of "Naval Parachutist" when they complete this phase of SQT.

Various types of communications equipment and extensive medical skills and life-saving techniques that have proven essential during combat operations are covered. This phase also includes cold-weather training in Alaska as well as more extensive training in waterborne operations.

Upon the successful completion of SQT, students are finally awarded the coveted Trident insignia and they are designated as fully qualified Navy SEALs. Each individual will be assigned to an operational unit, where they will undergo more advanced training and, of course, will deploy with their units on various training and contingency operations.

BUD/S and Hell Week

Now that you have a basic understanding of the training pipeline all SEALs have to undergo before becoming a fully qualified frogman, it is important that you gain a deeper appreciation of BUD/S and what occurs there so you'll stand a better chance at understanding Navy SEALs. More importantly, you will gain a better understanding of the mindset and mental approach that encompasses the iron will that enables SEALs to do what they do best—produce exceptional results in exceptionally challenging environments and situations.

As you continue reading you will come to understand that within special operations units in the U.S. and around the world, the terms *training* and *selection* have two very distinct and different meanings.

A *training course* is one in which students are educated and trained in specific concepts, skills, and techniques. For example, a SEAL attending the sniper course will learn the tactics and techniques associated with serving as a sniper.

A *selection course* is one that is designed to screen, test, and evaluate students for certain physical and mental attributes. In most special operations units, candidates must first pass selection before they are allowed to receive any measurable amount of training.

BUD/S is a hybrid of these concepts. It is a training course, which means the students are actually learning some of the skills and techniques associated with serving as a SEAL. It is also a selection course, which means that there's much more involved in becoming a SEAL than learning and performing the skills and techniques previously mentioned—it is about meeting standards, written and unwritten, that are the hurdles one must clear in order to wear the Trident. I think it is obvious that the BUD/S evolution known as Hell Week is more geared toward selection versus training!

Hell Week

This very short part of the course is perhaps the most fundamentally significant one in BUD/S. It consists of five and a half days of continuous gruelingly difficult activities designed to push the candidates to their absolute physical, mental, and emotional limits. Not only are they running, swimming, and maneuvering boats in frigid waters, but they are doing so with only a total of 4 hours of sleep throughout the entire evolution.

The main purpose of Hell Week is to screen out the students who lack the commitment or mental toughness to endure significant amounts of pain, discomfort, exhaustion, and stress. This is necessary because the academic and physical training that follows Hell Week becomes increasingly challenging. The instructors want to ensure that they have eliminated those who are not truly committed to serving as a SEAL. Typically, 75 percent of the students who start a BUD/S class fail to make it through training, and Hell Week is the most common event during which they fail.

Hell Week explodes unexpectedly, trainees know it will happen, but they don't know when. They only know it will start with chaos:

> *They ran us out of the tent, screaming: 'Go here, go over there, you guys can't get it right, drop on the ground, get up.' We were trying to do what they were telling us to do, but there was too much at once, it was impossible. They were*

> *spraying us with hoses, shooting off guns. 'Hit the ocean,' they ordered and we had to jump in the surf. It was a cold night, and we were freezing. After we were completely soaked, they hauled us back out and screamed at us to do push-ups, pull-ups, and sit-ups.*
> —Richard Machowicz, *Unleash the Warrior Within*

Throughout the week, be it day or night, the students remain in constant motion as they complete a series of training evolutions built around running, swimming, small boat races, crawling through foul-smelling mud flats, and a number of other events, contests, and situations designed to make the students physically miserable. This, in turn, leads them to wage a constant mental battle with themselves as they contemplate just how badly they want to be a SEAL.

After a couple of days of little to no sleep, combined with extremely high amounts of physical output, many of the students are disoriented and no longer know what day of the week it is. Their voices are hoarse from sounding off for the instructors. Some areas of their bodies have been chafed to the point of bleeding, from being in constant contact with wet sand, which seems to get into every crack and crevice of their bodies.

48 hours into Navy SEAL Richard Machowicz's Hell Week, the instructors put him and his comrades into the cold ocean once again. They brought out the ship's bell, and announced that they weren't going to let anybody out until somebody quits.

The class stayed in the water for 30 minutes, shivering from the cold. One guy couldn't take it anymore, he jumped up and rang the bell three times—he was out. A rush of people followed him, and the bell kept on ringing. In 10 minutes, 80 men dropped out of BUD/S Class 136.

To make matters worse, the instructors drove an ambulance in, filled with hot chocolate, coffee, and donuts, which they served to the quitters.

> ...Meanwhile, while it seemed our classmates were being rewarded for quitting, the few of us remaining in the water hadn't stopped shaking ... Somewhere in the corner of my mind came the realization that the instructors were weeding us out by playing negative games with our minds. The only way I would be able to win this one would be to play a positive game.
> —Richard Machowicz, *Unleash the Warrior Within*

As a result of sleep deprivation, it is quite common for students to hallucinate during Hell Week, and while the students are not really aware of this, the instructor staff remains vigilant to prevent students from seriously injuring themselves. Medical personnel are present throughout Hell Week, and they do their best to patch up students with minor injuries and get them back to their boat teams.

Most of the training evolutions conducted during Hell Week are competitive in nature, pitting one boat team against another. As is the case throughout BUD/S, the instructors reward the winners of these competitions. It is common for them to grant a winning boat team permission to lie down for 15 minutes of sleep or to allow them to stand close to a warm fire, while the losing teams are punished unmercifully.

During Hell Week the instructors constantly harass, ridicule, and taunt the students, often using bullhorns to broadcast their nonstop barrage of insults, sarcastic comments, and offers of "hot coffee and donuts" for those who have had enough and want to quit BUD/S. This, of course, is the main goal of the instructors—to get the mentally weak to cave in and ring the bell three times.

SEAL training is intense for a reason: it's designed to sift out the strong of spirit from the weak of will. As Dick Couch, a Navy SEAL veteran from the Vietnam era, wrote in *The Warrior Elite*:

> *SEAL training, beginning from day one at BUD/S, is designed to create warriors ... It is a sorting process that finds young men who would rather die than quit, then instills them with a relentless desire to fight and win as a team ... It is a ruthless process; for every man who succeeds, four men will fail. It's a rendering for men of character, spirit, and a burning desire to win at all costs.*
> —Dick Couch, *The Warrior Elite*

How do these young men weather such brutal training, brave through the terrors of Hell Week, and endure to graduate as Navy SEALs in the end?

> *While you have to be physically strong to survive BUD/S, you also have to be mentally and emotionally resilient.*
>
> *Hell Week isn't designed to kill you. It's designed to make you wish you were dead—or at least to push you to the edge of physical and*

mental endurance to see how you react. While the demands are mostly physical, the journey through them is all about mental attitude.
—Rorke Denver, Damn Few

BUD/S students often mistakenly believe that Hell Week is all about physical strength and endurance, but those who manage to survive it and continue on to become SEALs say that mental toughness is the critical factor required to get through this evolution. Once they pass Hell Week, the vast majority of students will indeed go on to become fully qualified SEALs.

BUD/S will quickly weed out those who lack both the physical capability and the level of commitment needed to succeed as a SEAL. It usually takes longer, however, to identify and eliminate those who are physically capable of serving as SEALs and who truly want to do so, but are lacking the strength of will and mental toughness to serve as SEAL Team guys. Historically, those making it through Hell Week have a very high probability of making it through the entire pipeline and becoming SEALs, but there have been cases where men who survive Hell Week ultimately fail to complete BUD/S. I once heard a BUD/S instructor say, "The millstone of BUD/S grinds slowly, but it grinds finely." I thought this to be a profound statement then, and still do today.

Men are very rarely dismissed from a BUD/S class; instead, they are continuously pushed to their mental and physical limits until some of them choose to quit the course. BUD/S is a course full of traditions, customs, and rituals and even the act of quitting has evolved into a standardized routine. Quitting, or *dropping on request* (DOR) is done through a public event called "Ringing Out." When a trainee decides that he can't go on and decides to quit, he rings a large brass bell three times and places his helmet on the deck alongside those of former classmates who have already exited the course. Men who ring out of BUD/S are not harassed or demeaned by the instructor staff. They are quickly removed from the training area and processed for orders to another duty station where they will complete their time in the Navy.

In the final analysis, BUD/S takes men possessing the raw aptitude and traits to serve as a frogman, and through training and time develops them into men with a very powerful mindset—an invincible mentality that is always focused on finding a way to succeed. The purpose of BUD/S is to instill some of the fundamental core values of the SEAL community into the students. These core values include:

- Accomplishing the mission is all that matters.
- They don't hand out 2nd Place trophies in war.
- Whatever needs to happen, must be *made* to happen.
- Luck is good, but preparation is better.
- Never make excuses.
- One must never bring shame to the SEAL brotherhood.

In order to fulfill these values and deliver upon their promise, SEALs are put through an incredibly difficult trial that calls for an extraordinary amount of mental toughness. Although most SEALs possess mental toughness as they initiate this training, it is through strife, pain and perseverance that this mental fortitude is brought to the level needed for these men to successfully and effectively function in the scenarios that SEALs are invariably placed under.

If we take some of the same methods used by SEALs and apply them in our own quest for optimal performance in our lives, this mental toughness is a malleable clay that any one of us can mold into the masterpiece that will give us the needed edge in order to accomplish any goal.

Earn Your Trident Every Day

"By wearing the Trident I accept the responsibility of my chosen profession and way of life. It is a privilege that I must earn every day." These words taken from the SEAL Ethos allude to the philosophy of the SEAL community that no SEAL can ever rest on his laurels or be satisfied with his current level of knowledge, skill, physical fitness, or any other aspect of serving as a Navy SEAL. This philosophy has been summarized in a statement known to all SEALs—Earn *Your Trident Every Day!*

This statement, as powerful as it is brief, reminds every SEAL that there is always something that he can do to improve, and that in the SEAL community, continuous improvement is something that is expected. It is simply what SEALs do, and it applies to everything they do, for as long as they live.

"Earn Your Trident Everyday" means that every day one must push past the limits of yesterday's performance or achievements. It means turning weaknesses into strengths and strengths into superior capabilities. It implies that perfection is the goal; and that at the end of every day every SEAL must be able to reflect that he did everything possible to improve himself and, by extension, his beloved SEAL brotherhood.

Despite the grueling training a newly-designated SEAL has undergone by the time he reports into his first operational unit, he still has a long way to go before his teammates are willing to put their lives in his hands. A new SEAL has much to learn and experience before he will be counted amongst the proven and seasoned SEALs in a unit. The traditional "welcome aboard" reception that awaits new SEALs has evolved over time as a way of impressing upon them that even though they now wear the Trident, they are still new and can't be fully accepted as operators in the fullest sense. Enlisted or officer, every new SEAL will once again face a series of "evolutions," except that unlike those in BUD/S and SQT, these evolutions and tests are, for the most part, unscripted and unscheduled, with the sole purpose of humbling the incoming rookies and reminding them that their journey as SEALs has just begun; that they indeed must earn their Trident every day!

Selection Is Continuous

In a previous chapter you learned the differences between military courses that are designed for training versus selection purposes. Every major special operations unit in the world has some form of selection process that serves as the gate through which one must pass in order to become a member of the unit. As in the SEAL teams, members of these units soon realize that the hard work and evaluation process doesn't end with passing the selection process. In other words, if getting into the unit was hard, remaining in it is even harder!

"Selection is continuous" is a phrase utilized to signify that the testing will continue. Whether referring to an exceptionally arduous training evolution, or simply referring to the fact that all newbies are at the bottom of the pecking order in the unit, it means that you will continue to be measured against the other SEALs or even against yourself on a daily basis. If you are to truly understand how SEALs think and approach life, you must carefully study and reflect upon what you are about to read in this chapter.

Why SEALs Continuously Test Themselves

The journey to becoming a SEAL is a long and difficult one. So difficult, that 75% of those who enter the training pipeline fail to successfully complete it. It is a well-known fact that the training will often be physically and emotionally brutal. Why then, do so many young men subject themselves to such agony?

One psychologist working within the Naval Special Warfare community told me, "The men who desire to become SEALs have an innate thirst for high-achievement. They want to separate themselves from other men by way of their accomplishments and by achieving things that most cannot." He went on to say that most high-achievers in sports, the business world, science and academia, automobile racing, etc., share a common need for excitement and the surge of adrenaline that is associated with performing at the outer limits of whatever it is they are doing at the time. Studies have shown that the levels of adrenaline, endorphins, and other "feel good" substances produced by the human body are as comparable in stock traders on the floor of the New York Stock Exchange, doctors performing lengthy surgical procedures, and salesmen pitching their product or services to high-level executives, as they are to those found in extreme athletes or military personnel engaging in high-risk operations. In other words, SEALs, like most high-achievers, crave the excitement associated with taking on significant challenges, including ones that involve the risk of death or serious injury.

"We want to be in a situation under maximum pressure, maximum intensity, and maximum danger. When it is shared with others, it provides a bond which is stronger than any tie that can exist."
—*SEAL Team Six Officer*

"It's a mindset that is prevalent in the SEAL community," said the psychologist, who has worked with SEALs for almost a decade. "What you have is a bunch of highly trained, very capable men who don't seem happy unless they are being measured or evaluated in some way, by others or by themselves. The higher the standard they are being judged against, the better." He went on to say, "Most outsiders would think that once a man becomes a SEAL and joins a team, he's able to relax a bit and enjoy his newly-acquired status as a member of an elite group of warriors. That's not what happens. Instead, newly minted SEALs discover that while they are now wearing the same highly coveted Trident insignia as their more seasoned teammates, they are being looked at as unknown quantities and must prove themselves worthy of being trusted with the lives of those who have been operating as SEALs for a decade or longer. It is part of what makes the SEALs unique; the test is never over and you have to earn your Trident every day."

What Motivates SEALs

Why do the vast majority of SEALs continuously seek to push themselves beyond established limits, when most people are content to settle for far less demanding lives? Here's the psychologist's response, "It's the innate need for achievement that is shared by most SEALs, the accomplishment of goals, specifically, exceptionally demanding goals that are typically seen as unattainable by most people. Coming in as a close second motivator is the competitive factor. SEALs love to win and the only way one is able to win is to compete. The competition can be against fellow SEALs, or anyone for that matter; but I can assure you that if a SEAL is in a room with at least one other person, he's competing in some way against that person, even if that person isn't aware of it!"

Studies of top level achievers in various professions and competitive environments such as world-class sports depict the same need for success and attainment of lofty goals, and a sheer love of competing against someone or some type of measurable standard. For SEALs, whether the goal is to become the best sniper in his unit or finishing a night land navigation exercise in record time, achieving success with a competitive edge is the sought after prize. They enjoy knowing that they are among the few who have dreamed of living the life of a SEAL, and actually achieved the dream.

"It's a sense of identity," said one SEAL. "The SEAL community is very small. There aren't many men who have the ability to continuously train and push themselves to the degree that we do. Professional athletes earn a lot of money and fame, but to be honest, I'd rather have the feeling of knowing that I'm living a life (as a SEAL) that very few men can live."

The Adrenaline Factor

The adrenaline factor likely plays a role in explaining why SEALs constantly seek to test themselves against the outer limits of various physical and mental skills and challenges. An "adrenaline surge" courses through the body when the adrenal glands are stimulated through heightened activity or other stressors. This surge is part of the release of a number of hormones, including adrenaline. For many SEALs, this feeling is one that they cannot get enough of.

"A lot of SEALs openly admit that they are seeking that rush," says a Navy psychologist who has worked with the SEAL community. "They're looking for those sensations they get from putting their life on the line during dangerous training evolutions or even actual combat operations. For many, it is a feeling that they cannot get elsewhere—a feeling of acute awareness and crystal-clear focus, of knowing they are exceeding expectations. They either succeed and live—or they die. It's very much a primitive thing, but SEALs love it and they seek it out at every opportunity."

Pushing the Limits

Why do the vast majority of SEALs feel a need to push themselves to the next level, closer to the edge of established barriers and limits? Why is it that their last accomplishment is never good enough?

"SEALs say that it simply isn't rewarding to repeatedly accomplish the same goals or conquer the same challenges, even if they are quite significant and perhaps even dangerous," says the psychologist. "Performing the same activities and doing well at them simply doesn't bring the same amount of excitement as it did the first time, so they want to push themselves even farther and go for the next big goal."

He went on to say, "It is a mindset that men who are drawn to the SEAL community are risk takers. This trait, combined with a love of pushing themselves past previous physical and mental limits, is what makes SEALs unique as individuals. When you have a few hundred of them assigned to the same SEAL team, what you get is a group of high-achievers who are constantly competing against each other. The result is what you'd expect—a high-testosterone ultra-competitive group of winners who revel in testing themselves against any and all opponents and challenges."

SEAL Missions

The previous chapters have presented a brief introduction to the type of initial training Navy SEALs participate in. I would like to now introduce you to some of the types of missions these men routinely perform, both during training and during actual operations.

It can't be denied that being physically fit is a prerequisite in order to be a Navy SEAL. However, physical fitness is NOT the most important trait that is needed. This may come as a surprise to some of you, but there are many other qualities that are paramount if you are to succeed the life of a Navy SEAL. An unwavering iron will, resolve, tenacity, and mental toughness are all attributes necessary for these men to be able to conduct the types of missions that they do, and to persevere in the types of environments in which they operate and the life-and-death situations they often face. Combat is not a competition—you are not there to compete, you are there to dominate and overwhelm the enemy, otherwise you won't be coming home.

During an interview on a nationally-televised talk-show, the host of the show was discussing with a Navy SEAL the various countries he had been sent to during his career. She was quite impressed that this SEAL had been to so many different places around the world, however, she was completely missing the main reason behind his travels. This brief exchange, which happened during the interview, brought to the show's host an immediate focus on the reality of what SEALs do, and I thought it was worth sharing.

Interviewer: "Did you have to learn several languages?"

Navy SEAL: "No, ma'am, we don't go there to talk."

Interviewer: "Oh...I see...ok."

It is important that you understand that Navy SEALs exist for one purpose—as implied by the comment made by the SEAL during that interview—to <u>kill the enemies of the United States.</u>

Sound cruel or barbaric? Perhaps... but it is also reality. The cold, hard truth is that the battlefield is often associated with conditions and actions that most people would consider savage or uncivilized. The battlefield isn't at all like the sports arena or the business world—it is combat, and it usually means death for someone. If you walk onto a battlefield only looking to compete with the enemy, more than likely you will be that someone who ends up dying. No one walks off a battlefield unscathed, you may walk away bloodied, bruised, and battered, but alive; it all depends on the training and the mindset with which you begin the battle. The competitive nature of Navy SEALs is one of the factors that usually dictates a winning outcome when they operate.

Developing an attitude of "domination versus competition" begins from the moment they start their preparation for selection, and it is infused into the entire culture of the Teams. Everyone associated with the SEAL community, be they SEALs or support personnel, operates with a mindset of "maxing out" and achieving excellence in everything that they do. This mindset stems from the early lessons all SEALs learn at BUD/S, where students are constantly reminded that *"It Pays to be A Winner!"* This mindset is developed through various forms of competition and brutally difficult training. Through the various methods utilized by the instructors, and later on the members of a SEAL unit, the mentality of trainees and SEALs starting out is transformed and shaped into that of a warrior who perseveres against all odds and relentlessly seeks to dominate the enemy and any other factor that might threaten the successful accomplishment of the mission.

I know that the vast majority of people reading this book will have no association with the military, and therefore have no chance of actually going to war in the literal sense. But, as stated previously, the mission of the book is to help you understand the mindset and invincible mentality that infuse the iron will of Navy SEALs. To do so, one must always remember why the SEAL teams exist and why the training to become a SEAL is so difficult.

Much of the information contained in this chapter was extracted from a research study conducted by the Naval Special Warfare Command. The purpose of the study was to identify physically demanding missions and mission segments performed during SEAL operations and to rank them according to their importance to mission success. The ultimate objective was to identify the abilities that contribute to success as a SEAL operator. Not surprisingly, some personality traits and intellectual skills, such as problem solving, assertiveness, and the ability to work effectively as a member of a Team, emerged during interviews of several dozen highly experienced SEALs as being even more important to the probable success of a SEAL operator than many physical attributes and abilities.

The study results imply a need for high-levels of mental toughness in SEALs, which, of course, aligns with the main purpose of this book—learning about the mindset common to all SEALs.

Survey Results

Interviews of the veteran SEALs revealed 23 traits and abilities that were felt to be the primary factors associated with successful SEAL operators. It is important to note how many of the most important traits and skills, as defined by highly experienced SEALs, are mental versus physical. If you review, for example, the definitions for *teamwork* and *problem solving*, you'll quickly realize that there are many, perhaps dozens of associated traits and skills implied in each, almost all of which are mental attributes.

Most Important Traits (in order of importance according to the study)

- **Teamwork:** The ability to work with others as part of a team, to anticipate what others want or need, and to cooperate.
- **Stamina:** The ability to maintain physical activity over prolonged periods of time.
- **Problem Solving:** The ability to perceive small details and "size-up" situations quickly and accurately, and then respond with an appropriate course of action.
- **Reaction Time:** The speed with which a single motor response can be made following the onset of a single stimulus.
- **Assertiveness:** The ability to bring a problem or important information to the attention of another crew member in a timely fashion.
- **Strength:** The amount of muscular force that can be exerted.
- **Night Vision:** The ability to see under low light conditions.
- **Memorization:** The ability to remember information, such as words, numbers, pictures, and procedures.

Important Traits (in order of importance according to the study)

- **Peripheral Vision:** The ability to perceive objects or movement towards the edges of the visual field.
- **Depth Perception:** The ability to distinguish which of several objects is nearer or more distant, or to judge the distance to an object.
- **Manual Dexterity:** The ability to make skillful, coordinated movements of a hand together with its arm--may involve equipment, but not equipment controls.
- **Oral Comprehension:** The ability to understand spoken English words or sentences.
- **Far Vision:** The ability to see distant environmental surroundings.
- **Near Vision:** The ability to see close environmental surroundings.
- **Arm-Hand Steadiness:** The ability to make precise, steady arm-hand positioning movements
- **Oral Expression:** The ability to speak English words or sentences so others will understand.
- **Speed of Limb Movement:** The speed with which movements of the arms or legs can be made; the speed

with which the movement can be carried out after it has been initiated.

- **Finger Dexterity:** The ability to make skillful, coordinated movements of the fingers--may involve equipment, but not equipment controls.
- **Color Discrimination:** The ability to match or discriminate between colors.
- **Written Comprehension:** The ability to understand written sentences and paragraphs.
- **Control Precision:** The ability to make fine adjustments to a knob or dial
- **Math Reasoning:** The ability to understand and organize a problem and then to select a mathematical method or formula to solve the problem.
- **Written Expression:** The ability to write English words or sentences so others will understand.

SEAL Missions and Physical Tasks

The research study produced a long list of missions, mission segments, and physical tasks associated with SEAL operations. I selected a number of them for inclusion in this chapter as a means of introducing you to the physical demands placed on SEAL operators. Reviewing this material will also better enable you to contemplate the mindset and attitude necessary for nearly continuous participation in high-risk, dangerous and physically demanding operations.

As you review these missions and physical tasks, you'll note that many are associated with walking long distances in extreme weather conditions while bearing heavy loads of equipment, including ammunition and explosives. Some require surface swimming for many miles in frigid waters in both daylight and darkness; and others entail several hours of sub-surface, clandestine infiltration of an enemy controlled area to emplace mines, conduct direct action missions, or to perform various reconnaissance-related activities.

I've only listed about 50% of the missions and physical tasks that were included in the study. I contemplated limiting what I showed here even more, for brevity's sake, but decided that the more readers could learn about SEAL operations, the better they could understand the mindset that is associated with these warriors. I doubt that anyone can read what follows and not be impressed by the magnitude of what America demands of its naval commandos. Likewise, learning more about what SEALs do on a frequent basis will allow you to fully understand why the physical and mental standards associated with joining the SEAL community are so high.

I don't think anyone could argue, after reading this material, that it takes a special breed of man to be able to endure such extreme environments, withstand such punishing conditions, bear such strenuous loads, while at the same time executing difficult tasks; oh, and let's not forget, possibly fighting off an enemy and trying to stay alive—they do this day after day, constantly and continuously.

None of the material you are about to read is classified or otherwise sensitive information from a military intelligence or operational security perspective, it has all been cleared by appropriate authorities for public dissemination. That said, an astute reader will note the absence of specific missions and physical tasks more closely aligned with recent SEAL operations in Iraq and Afghanistan. Much has been learned over the past thirteen years of operating in these challenging environments, resulting in the modification and enhancement of several training techniques and programs.

Navy SEAL Missions and Physical Tasks

- Walk 9 miles over uneven terrain at night, carrying a 125lb. pack (including radios and other gear), in 70°F temperature, to objective; then, retrace steps to extraction point.
- Serve as point man (trail breaker) for an element walking a distance of 26 miles through dense jungle (up and down), in tropical heat and humidity, during a 3 day period, carrying a 60 lbs. pack and weapons.
- Perform a "duck drop," followed by a 21 mile transit (3 hours) in 48°F air temperature, then swim a distance of 2,000 meters in 56°F water carrying a limpet mine and using a Drager underwater breathing apparatus (UBA); return to Zodiac without limpet, then travel 4 miles to extraction point (10 hours total).
- Walk a distance of 26 miles through dense jungle terrain (up and down), in tropical heat and humidity, during a 3 day period, carrying a 40lb. pack, an M-60 (17 lbs.), and 400 rounds of ammunition (40 lbs.).
- Perform a "duck drop," followed by a 14 mile transit in moderate seas and 65°F air temperature; beach and cache boat, and proceed on foot over 200 meters of strand; enter water and swim 3 miles in current to objective;

then, retrace steps to insertion point, during an 8-hour period.

- Travel for 5 hours in an open rubber boat in 40°F air temperature and 30-foot swells; beach the boat, cache/stage the equipment, and change from dry suit into dry clothes; then walk 16 miles during the next 2 nights over uneven terrain carrying an 80lb. pack, sleeping in 2-hour increments, when possible, during a continuous rain.

- Walk a distance of 35 miles from sea level to 4,000 feet, traversing marshy and rocky terrain (frequently on incline below the ridge line), walking at night and laying up during the day, for 3 days, carrying an 80lb. pack, in 30°F to 70°F air temperature.

- Perform a "duck drop" into 39°F water, then conduct a 57 mile over-the-horizon boat transit, then a 2 hour ship attack wearing wet suit and Drager UBA; then, reboard Zodiac for 50 miles, ride to the extraction point.

- Lock out of a submerged submarine, then conduct a 70 mile over-the-horizon transit in a Zodiac in 65°F air temperature (5 hours); enter 58°F water wearing wet suit and Drager UBA, then swim a multi-ship limpet attack that requires 3 1/2 hours under water, re-board Zodiac for 70 mile ride to the extraction point.

- Walk a distance of 12 miles over uneven, snow-covered terrain in 30°F air temperature (crossing two 20-foot streams) during a 2-day period, wearing snowshoes and winter gear, and carrying an 80lb. pack.
- Launch and operate a SEAL delivery vehicle (SDV) for a period of 2 hours, then bottom-out the craft, swim 200 meters to shore carrying 90lbs. of equipment and weights and wearing a dry suit, then proceed overland 1.86 miles to objective; retrace steps to extraction point.
- Walk 37 miles through the desert during a 5-day period, carrying a 100lb rucksack, laying up during the day in 112°F temperature and walking over uneven terrain during nighttime hours (95°F).
- Perform a "duck drop" into 30°F waters then transit 76 miles in a rigid inflatable boat while wearing a dry suit; enter water and swim 600 meters through surf zone to beach while carrying a 50lb pack and weapons; cache boats and change from dry suit to winter gear on beach; hike 2 miles up steep incline with packs; then hike all night for the next 5 nights, laying up during daylight; then, periodically help other platoon members carry

downed pilot on stretcher over uneven terrain to extraction point.

- Travel for 6 hours in a Zodiac in 0°F air temperature, then swim 600 meters in 36°F water, crossing the surf zone to the beach; change from wetsuit into winter gear and snow shoes, then walk 1.2 miles over uneven terrain and snow to objective; retrace steps to extraction point (24 hours total).
- Walk a distance of 8 miles through dense jungle (up and down), in tropical heat and humidity, carrying a 40lb pack, an M-60 (17 lbs.), and 400 rounds of ammunition (40 lbs.).
- Perform a rescue drag of a wounded comrade weighing 170 lbs., dragging him by the web gear a distance of 75 meters, with the assistance of 1 other SEAL.
- Climb a 3-tier caving ladder (90 feet) wearing full close quarter battle (CQB) gear and carrying 25 lbs. of weapons and ammunition, pulling self and equipment onto deck of a steel structure.
- Carry a disabled comrade (weighing 170 lbs.) a distance of 200 meters, with the assistance of 2 other SEALs.
- Carry an unconscious SEAL 100 meters through jungle, across 50 feet of sandy beach to water, inflate his

flotation device, then tow him seaward for the next 2 hours until rescued.

- Carry a disabled comrade (weighing 170 lbs.) a distance of 500 meters, using a makeshift stretcher, with the assistance of 3 other SEALs.
- Carry a downed and disabled pilot (weighing 170 lbs.) a distance of 100 feet across a beach and through the surf zone.
- Fast rope from an altitude of 50 feet to the heaving deck of a ship while wearing close quarter battle (CQB) gear and carrying 50 lbs. of equipment and weapons.
- Ride in a CRRC for 1 hour to reach a sandy beach; cache the boat and proceed through thick jungle for 500 yards until coming under fire from a numerically superior enemy force; return fire and call in naval gunfire support; return to CRRC to prevent encirclement; then, quickly return to the engagement area through heavy fire to retrieve a critically injured comrade; carry the unconscious SEAL back to the beach, inflate his lifejacket, then tow him seaward for the next 2 hours until picked up by support craft.
- Conduct R&S for 5 days in a jungle environment (95°F temperature and high humidity), while carrying 60 lbs.

of equipment and a sniper rifle (movement restricted by thick vegetation to 50 meters per hour.)

- Ride for 3 hours in a riverine patrol boat, then for 1 hour in a CRRC on a jungle river (85°F air temperature and high humidity); climb a 350 foot cliff carrying a rifle and 20 lbs. of ammunition; descend 200 feet through dense vegetation; avoid, return, and eventually suppress intense enemy fire; then, carry wounded comrade 200 yards to extraction site with the assistance of 2 other SEALs.

- Operate a sampan on a jungle river for 4 hours at night; hike through uneven jungle terrain for 1 hour carrying light weapons; locate downed pilot and carry him back to the river with the assistance of 1 other person; return down river for 3 hours then evade intense machine gun fire, direct an air strike to suppress the fire, and successfully reach a forward operating base with the rescued pilot.

- Swim on surface a distance of 3.5 miles wearing full close quarter battle (CQB) gear and flotation device and carrying 25 lbs. of weapons/ammunition, in 60°F water; cling to the barnacle-covered leg of an oil platform for 45 minutes (while lead climber scales the structure); then climb a 3 tier caving ladder (90 feet), quietly pulling self and equipment onto deck of platform.

- Crawl for 3 days through a rat and mosquito infested jungle in 90°F temperature and 100% humidity, while carrying a 50lb pack and 25 lbs. of weapons and ammunition; lay up for 2 days, conduct sniper attack, then run .62 miles to extraction point.

- Fast rope to the deck of a salvage ship with 60 lbs. of equipment, then load 6 personnel and their equipment into 2 Zodiacs and launch the boats into 4-foot seas (30°F and 20 kt winds--all personnel wearing dry suits); proceed for 60 miles (10 hours) then take the boats through the surf, caching 1 on the beach (while the other craft and 2 personnel depart); then hump 6.2 miles over uneven terrain with 3 other SEALs (carrying 60 lbs. of equipment each); lay-up for 6 hours, then retrace steps (i.e., 6.2 mile hump, boat through surf zone, and 10 hour ride to extraction point).

- Conduct a 12 day final training exercise in -15°F temperature, covering 37 miles on skis while carrying a 100lb pack.

- Serve as mission specialist riding in an SDV for a period of 3 hours in 68°F water, while wearing a wet suit and

MK 15/16 UBA (from an offshore location to within an enemy harbor that is filled with jelly fish); open canopy then swim 50 meters to target to deploy limpets (while jelly fish repeatedly sting exposed lip area); return to SDV and sit among jelly fish in storage compartment as the SDV is operated out of the harbor to the rendezvous location (a total of 8 hours in 68°F water--2 hours of which is in jellyfish infested waters).

- Parachute (static line) into the desert with 150lb packs (day temp 110°F), then walk 47 miles during the next 7 nights.
- Serve as mission specialist riding in an SDV for a period of 3 hours in 65°F water, while wearing a light wet suit; exit SDV then swim 100 meters to shore; change into dry clothes then hump 1.2 miles with 50lb packs in 75°F air temperature; lay up overnight, then hump back to the beach for a 5-hour Zodiac extraction (a total of 2 days with only 3 quarts of water for each person).
- Hike 68 miles in winter gear, carrying a 60lb pack and weapons and completing 5 mini FTXs during a 6 day period (in 25°F temperature with continuous rain and snow). (19%)

- Ride in a Zodiac 6 miles to a rocky beach in 0°F air temperature while wearing winter gear; then, during the next 9 days traverse 50 miles of countryside (uneven terrain, briar patches) by humping (80% of the distance) and cross-country skiing (20%), while carrying a 100lb pack and weapons.
- Parachute into 42°F water wearing wet suits and Drager UBA; tread water for 4 hours waiting for small diesel submarine; enter submerged submarine; travel for 3 days in submarine, then lock out and swim 2 miles on the surface followed by 4 miles underwater (4 hour dive); crawl across 100 meters of rock quay, then swim 3 miles on surface to extraction point.
- Walk 72 miles in 2 1/2 days carrying an M-60, 600 rounds of ammunition, and a rucksack (90 lbs. total), laying up during the day (35°F temp at night and 80°F during the day).
- Perform a "duck drop" from an altitude of 65 feet; repair deflated section of Zodiac, then proceed 40 miles to shore; change into dry clothing and cache boats; swim 1.25 miles (in patrol clothes) towing 30 lbs. of equipment; then climb a 250 foot cliff; remain on top for

2 days, then retrace steps to extraction point (50°F air temperature).

- Perform a "soft-duck drop" then transit 35 miles to surf zone; guide boat through 5 foot surf to shore, then push the boat along the shore line for 8 miles with 3 other SEALs; lay up for 4 days in the jungle, then drive the boat 16 miles to pick up 4 personnel and 800 lbs. of gear; return at slow speed (requiring 8 hours to go the 16 miles), then recon the target for 4 more days before extraction.

- Parachute onto a rocky island then walk 1.2 miles over uneven terrain to shore; retrieve cached kayak, then travel 20 miles in rough seas to objective; travel 6 more miles in kayak, then climb a 2,500-foot mountain (mud and rocks) to the extraction point.

- Navigate a rigid inflatable boat for 10 hours through heavy seas (30°F) with no moon while wearing a dry suit; retrieve personnel who were washed out of boat; fall out of boat and cling to outboard motor (which is operating); climb back into boat and continue operating it; crash boat on rocks, then swim 200 meters through surf zone to beach carrying a 40lb pack and weapons; change into light Goretex outwear (winter gear was lost on rocks) then hump 7 miles over uneven terrain carrying packs and weapons; spend 2 days ashore hiking during the night and laying up during the day, with little sleep, in 35°F air temperature, wind and rain; finally, extraction by vehicle.

It would be safe to say that it takes an immeasurable amount of determination, perseverance, discipline, and mental toughness to make it through even the shortest of these missions. All of these men feel the extreme heat and cold, exhaustion, fear, and pain that any human would feel under those conditions; the difference is that through the incredibly rigorous training that they put their bodies *and minds* through, they have reached that "next level" of fortitude. You can also elevate your mental toughness and level of resolve to such high-levels. I won't tell you it's easy, I won't tell you it won't take long, but what I can tell you is that IT CAN BE DONE!

What's Your Battlefield?

Assuming that you are not serving in the military or law enforcement, chances are that your battlefield is a bit more sedate and safe than the environments SEALs operate in—and that's a good thing! For many reading this book, the battlefield is the business world, while for others it may be associated with academia or athletics. For many, the battle is happening in their minds as they try to cope with the challenges of health issues or personal relationships. Whatever your particular battle is—your goal—no matter where it will be fought, the main concept that is woven throughout this book is that you should approach it as a SEAL would: Utterly dominate the battle through hard work, intelligent and consistent preparation, confidence, and focused actions.

Mental Toughness

The definition of *mental toughness* is elusive at best; it is known by many names and thought of in various ways, but it all comes down to the same meaning. It is that inner strength that resides somewhere in the depths of our minds, which takes over when the conscious and rational parts of our brain decides that we've had enough and it is time to let go of the reigns. Any will to go on is powered by that force, and once it sparks up it engulfs our entire being until we emerge triumphant. That strength, that force—that's Mental Toughness.

In an effort to learn more about the mindset and the personality traits that are more common among the high achieving few, many great sports psychologists have conducted several detailed studies. I think that some of their findings and opinions describe the type of mental toughness that you will need if you decide to become a Navy SEAL.

One highly-regarded sports psychologist, Dr. Jim Loehr of the Human Performance Institute defined mental toughness as follows:

> *Mental toughness is the ability to consistently perform towards the upper range of your talent and skill regardless of competitive circumstances. It is all about improving your mind so that it's always on your side; not sometimes helping you nor working against you as we all know it's quite capable of doing.*

In a research paper titled *What Is This Thing Called Mental Toughness? An Investigation of Elite Sport Performers*, authors Graham Jones, Sheldon Hanton and Declan Connaughton declared that mental toughness is:

> *Having the natural or developed psychological edge that enables you to: generally, cope better than your opponents with the many demands (competition, training, lifestyle) that sport places on a performer; specifically, be more consistent and better than your opponents in remaining determined, focused, confident, and in control under pressure.*

Lieutenant Commander Eric Potterat, Ph.D., a Naval Special Warfare Command psychologist, quotes Hamlet on the subject: "There is nothing either good or bad, but thinking makes it so."

Dr. Potterat relates this study to sports and described the difference between winners and losers:

Physically, there's very little difference between athletes who win Olympic gold and the rest of the field. It's like the SEAL candidates we see here. Terrific hardware. Situps, pushups, running, swimming — off the charts, superhuman. But over at the Olympic center, the sports psychologists found that the difference between a medal and no medal is determined by an athlete's mental ability. The elite athletes, the Tiger Woodses, the Kobe Bryants, the Michael Jordans — this is what separates them from the competition. Knowing how to use information.

Just about every Navy SEAL who made it through agrees that, ultimately, what determines whether you succeed or fail depends on whether you win the inner battle that rages and makes you question *"How much do I really want this?"* This question will be one that will run through you mind several times if you decide to go through the Navy SEAL selection courses.

Mental Toughness for Navy SEALs

A Navy SEAL officer conducted interviews with several members of the various SOF units on the topic of mental toughness and how it results in successfully conducting missions and overcoming challenges.

One of the questions asked of the operators was their definition of the term *mental toughness*. The SEAL responses are listed below. Keep in mind that because of the nature of their profession, some of their comments refer to loss of life during battle.

While reading their comments, ask yourself which statements align with what you already believe about mental toughness and which are new; and how this information might apply to your outlook and philosophies regarding your goal of becoming mentally tougher, more resilient, and more self-confident.

Navy SEAL Responses on the Meaning of Mental Toughness:

- Having unshakable confidence in your ability to achieve your goals.

- Knowing that you possess unique qualities and abilities that make you better than your opponents.

- Having an insatiable desire to succeed.

- Being resilient and able to quickly recover from adversity, disappointment, set-backs, etc.

- Thriving on the pressure of high-stakes events, including combat operations.

- Accepting that fear and anxiety are inevitable and knowing that you can overcome both.

- Able to remain fully focused on the mission.

- Remaining fully focused on the task at hand in the face of life-threatening situations.

- Being able to cope with high levels of physical and emotional pain, while still maintaining the ability to execute skills and tasks required to accomplish the mission.

- Quickly regaining psychological control following unexpected, uncontrollable events such as the death of a unit member during combat.

Traits Specific to Mental Toughness

Motivation, confidence, focus, composure, and resilience were among the most common traits mentioned by the men who were interviewed. These qualities, as you can imagine, are necessary for any operator to be an effective member of a unit; it is mental toughness and a high degree of emotional control, along with incessant special training, that enables Navy SEALs to remain composed, confident, and focused in order to be able to cope with fear and anxiety during combat operations.

Motivation

"Mission accomplishment" is the motivator that keeps you moving toward its achievement. Visualizing reaching that finish line will propel you to focus on the steps needed to get there.

Ask yourself *"Why do I want to be a Navy SEAL?"* or *"Why is it important that I achieve this goal?"* Figuring out the answers to those questions, will enable you to better understand your motivations and desires, which can lead to an even greater desire to achieve your goal, and more clearly defined objectives.

Confidence

Confidence is the knowledge that you possess the skills necessary to confront obstacles and successfully maneuver past them. It also enables you to bounce back after setbacks, mistakes or poor performances.

Because of their training regiment, Navy SEALs typically have an unshakeable confidence in their abilities. The harshness and intensity of the BUD/S training course, as well as all the subsequent training throughout a Navy SEAL's time as an operator, gives them confidence in their skills and "game plan," and in their ability to execute the plan during stressful, high-pressure situations.

Developing any skill requires a great deal of practice. Confidence is gained through repeatedly putting yourself through difficult scenarios that force you to utilize your skills to conquer the objective. Knowing that you've put in the time required to train and study properly prior to any task is a great confidence builder that you will need in order to make it through the program.

Focus

The ability to home in on what's most important at a given time and to be able to block out everything else, is a necessity for Navy SEALs to be able to carry out their missions.

This state of *hyper-focus* during the "Fog of War" that occurs during combat means focusing on what's most important at a given moment to accomplish the mission. It is a trait that will be very valuable as you ready yourself to undertake any challenge.

Composure

Composure is your ability to remain calm and in control and able to continue to perform at optimum levels, regardless of the situation. It is important that you understand that <u>the brain and mind are two separate things</u>. Your body obeys the brain, but the brain obeys the mind! There are certain emotions and reactions that are being produced by your brain's automatic responses to certain situations. Knowing these responses will occur enables you to cope with them by overriding your brain's signals and allowing your mind to control your actions.

Composure enables SEALs to have clarity of thought and focus during the heat of battle, and it promotes sound decision-making when the tactical situation requires rapid adjustments to established battle plans and mission orders.

During the initial SEAL training, candidates will constantly be confronted with situations that require them to use their minds (mental toughness) to overcome what their brains are telling your bodies. Their brains will sense that they are too cold or hot, or too injured to possibly pass the next graded event, etc. The men who quit are those who lose focus and composure and succumb to the messages the brain is sending, Those able to use their minds to remain composed continue to focus on the task at hand and simply do the very best they can at that moment. They use their minds to reach deep within themselves and find the strength to hang on and keep moving forward.

You will surely encounter situations during your personal and professional life in which your brain will tell you that you simply cannot continue on. You must resolve to ensure that your mind remains in control and enables you to stay focused and moving forward until you have overcome whatever challenge is facing you at that moment.

Resilience

Simply put, resilience is your unwillingness to give up. The obstacles and challenges Navy SEALs face in combat are difficult at best. The situations and environments their missions entail are often brutal. Having the ability to face them, bounce back from setbacks, and go on to succeed is paramount for mission accomplishment.

In order to succeed in life and accomplish challenging goals, you have to be willing to push through hardships, pain, and self-doubt. You simply have to be willing to never give up!

Life-long Mental Toughness

Once you begin to develop mental toughness for the purpose of achieving a specific goal, such as becoming a better business leader, student, parent or perhaps becoming more physically fit, it is a skill that will grow and continue to positively influence and benefit you throughout all stages of your life regardless of the environment you are operating in.

Mental toughness will also aid anyone struggling through "personal battles"—health issues, difficult situations at work; dealing with family or personal relationship problems; coping with depression, drug addiction, alcoholism or obesity.

These types of situations require a great amount of mental toughness in order to push past limitations, deal with the challenges facing you, and follow whatever steps are necessary to achieve your goals.

Essentially, mental toughness is a quality that is as critical to achieving your goals, assuming they are associated with a high-level of difficulty, stress and perhaps even various forms of risk. The most important thing to remember is that mental toughness can, in fact, be studied, developed, practiced and mastered!

Understanding Fear

The special operations community spends thousands of dollars as well as several years in order to train each individual to the level of proficiency required of their missions. For this reason the SOF leadership has become much more proactive in ensuring that this effort is not wasted, and that the members of their units remain physically, mentally, and emotionally fit for world-wide operations at a moment's notice.

These efforts include the study of various methods and techniques that are focused on the psychological well-being of Navy SEALS and other special operators. In order to develop these methods and design the appropriate training programs for their adaptation, the Navy leadership has dedicated teams for the purpose of studying fear, how it affects the human brain, and ways to combat these effects.

Studies conducted by psychologists reveal that "emotion" involves the entire nervous system. There are two parts of the nervous system, however, that mainly control our emotions and how our bodies react to them. These two parts are the Limbic System and the autonomic nervous system.

The Limbic System and Fear

The limbic system is a set of brain structures located on top of the brainstem and buried under the cortex, which mainly control our emotions—such as fear and anger—and motivations, particularly those that are related to survival.

Certain structures, the amygdala and the hippocampus, are limbic system structures that play important roles in memory. The amygdala is responsible for determining what memories are stored and where the memories are stored in the brain. It is thought that this determination is based on how huge an emotional response an event invokes.

The amygdala are two very small almond shaped masses of tissue on each side of the brain, which regulate emotional responses, hormonal secretions, and memory. The amygdala is responsible for fear conditioning or the associative learning process by which we learn to fear something.

The Autonomic Nervous System

The autonomic nervous system is made up of two parts, whose functions oppose or cancel out each other. The first is the **sympathetic nervous system**, which starts in the spinal cord and travels to a various parts of the body. It is responsible for preparing the body for the "fight or flight" reaction produced by awareness and fear of danger or threat.

The other part of the autonomic nervous system is called the **parasympathetic nervous system**. It extends from the brainstem to the spinal cord of the lower back. Its function is to bring the body back from the emergency status that the sympathetic nervous system puts it into.

The Physiology of Fear

Fear stimulates the sympathetic nervous system, which is responsible for the actions that our brains are programmed to execute when facing danger or threat. When the brain registers a situation that induces fear, it begins a chemical reaction in our bodies, sometimes referred to as the "fight-or-flight" reaction. The first thing that happens is an almost immediate release of a hormone called adrenaline (also known as the fight-or-flight hormone).

Imagine you are driving along, and suddenly two cars ahead of you collide forcing you to quickly slam on the brakes, dangerously change lanes, and decide what you are going to do—stop and help or say a prayer and keep driving. You will notice that your legs are suddenly shaking, your heart is racing, your palms are sweaty, and you are breathing very fast.

All these reactions in your body are the result of epinephrine, also known as adrenaline, having been released into your bloodstream. Adrenaline also causes a surge of energy or "arousal." Almost at the same time as adrenaline is released, the adrenal glands also release another hormone called norepinephrine. This hormone causes you to become more aware, more awake and better able to react to a stressful or threatening situation. It also shifts the blood flow from areas that may not be quite as necessary, like the skin or some internal organs such as the liver or kidneys, to others, such as your lungs and certain muscles, which would be essential for fleeing from danger. This is why you would probably feel a tingly feeling all over your body after a close-call-type event.

Finally, we have a chemical chain-reaction, which takes a few minutes, and that results in the release of cortisol into the blood. Cortisol regulates the fluid flow and the blood pressure in our bodies. All of the following reactions occur in our bodies as a response to fear or stress:

- Heart rate increases – in order to deliver more oxygen to the larger organs so they are ready to act.

- Pupils dilate - for better vision blood flow to the eyes is increased which also helps to open the eyelids wider.

- Bronchial tubes open up – in order to increase the intake or air and therefore oxygen so it can be delivered in the bloodstream to the bigger organs.

- Sweat glands are stimulated – in order to regulate the increase in heat your body is generating as a result of the increased blood flow to large muscle groups.

- Blood vessels in non-essential parts of the body become constricted - blood flow is being rerouted to the major muscle groups so fine motor skills become compromised, which causes tremors and shaking; the salivary gland are deactivated, which causes dry-mouth; secretions in the digestive system become inhibited, which causes a fluttering sensation (butterflies) or nausea; speech can become slurred; and dizziness may occur due to the increased breathing speed.

The natural response to fear can cause men in combat to lose the ability to perform the simplest of tasks (reloading their weapon, relocating to a covered position, etc.) and to become physically weak to the point that they cannot remain standing, or muster the strength to operate equipment or perform tasks that they've done successfully hundreds or thousands of times in the past. The Navy SEALs undergo extensive training to learn to overcome the effects of fear.

You should consider the fact that as you tackle difficult challenges, you will likely experience periods of great stress, anxiety, doubt and various degrees of fear. Understanding how fear affects the brain, and furthermore how your brain and body will react to fear and stress is essential to acquiring and developing methods to enhance the mental toughness and mindset necessary to override these natural reactions.

It is important to realize that your body never changes in this regard; it will always respond to threat-stress situations in the same way, producing some or all of the physical responses listed above. Through training, you can learn to anticipate these ever-present physiological and psychological responses and use various methods and techniques to control them.

Conquering Fear

The world has changed drastically since men lived in caves, hunted for their food, and fought for their daily survival. But despite the many ways our world has changed and the way we do things has changed, the body's physiological reactions to fear are much the same as those that our primitive ancestors experienced. No pill has been invented, and no technology has been created that can extinguish fear.

It is erroneous to think that Navy SEALs are able to function as they do because they are immune to fear. In actuality, it is the ability to anticipate situations that will initiate the body's coping mechanism for fear (the physiological responses listed in the previous chapter), that allows for the proper steps to be taken to negate the effects of these reactions.

Most situations that Navy SEALs face during combat will require that they be able to remain focused as they operate highly technical equipment, make rapid decisions and execute physical tasks that require both fine and gross motor skills. All SEALs must condition their minds to expect the fear-induced reactions in their bodies, and know how to neutralize their impact on human performance.

Mental Processes

There are some automatic processes that occur immediately upon becoming aware of a stressful event or situation; and they occur regardless of prior knowledge of the event. This is where the amygdala comes in and utilizes its memory storage and emotion regulation functions to decide whether to activate a "fight-or-flight" response.

First, we assess the situation and how it will affect us; then we assess how equipped we are to deal with the situation; and finally, we judge the consequences of either failure or success in handling the situation.

All of these processes occur almost instantaneously, in fractions of a second. After the processes have been concluded and our assessment has taken place, then the physiological responses to fear occur.

It is very important—for the purposes of controlling fear—that you clearly understand that a situation does not cause the emotional reaction, but rather it is the interpretation or meaning that our *mind* "assigns" to the situation that provokes the chain of events and reactions that result when fear is sensed. It all depends on whether the mind *perceives* that the individual is capable of coping with the situation or not.

Managing Fear

Fear can never be completely eradicated—at least not without surgically altering your brain—but it can be effectively controlled to maximize performance while facing a dangerous or threatening situation or event. It is critical that you also understand that it is a normal occurrence; feeling it does not in any way mean cowardice.

Openly discussing fear has been found to be an effective fear management tool for combat soldiers. Although most members of any special operations unit hate to admit weakness, they are now very familiar with the benefits of discussing fear before battle. It is simply another part of the mission. There is a saying that states: *"the man who knows he will be afraid and tries to get ready for it makes a better soldier,"* most combat-tested Navy SEALs agree with this sentiment.

The SEAL community wisely recognized that utilizing the information gained from various studies could enable them to enhance the performance of their operators, and as a result, all SEALs and support personnel now have access to psychologists and other medical professionals that are focused on helping them maintain a strong, resilient mindset.

The Navy SEAL Method of Conquering Fear

Fear research studies had a breakthrough when it revealed the discrepancy in the speed at which the amygdala receives information versus how fast it gets to the frontal lobes. The frontal lobes reside in the cortex of the brain, and they are where conscious, rational thought happens; it is the problem solving area.

It turns out that information gets to the amygdala at almost twice the speed as it gets to the frontal lobes. You can see how this would be a problem when it comes to controlling fear. If the brain signal that gives the fear alarm happens much faster than the brain signal that tells us how to react, then the result can be paralysis or panic. To avoid that it is important to *instinctively* know how to react to danger or threat.

The Naval Special Warfare community has freely shared extensive amounts of information regarding how Navy SEALs are trained to address their reactions to the human stress response.

Psychologists and neuroscientists now agree that fear can be conquered if you suppress the human response to it. To do this you must repeatedly confront your fears head on. Many of the Navy SEALs' training methods are based on this theory. For Navy SEALs, what most consider "courage" is achieved by facing the same difficult scenarios or dangerous environments on a daily basis. Throughout their training they perform the same complex and difficult exercises over and over, many times, until responses become automatic and the situation does not carry any emotional connection to the setting or the actions that ensue. They build up their immunity to it.

The repetitive and harsh nature of the training Navy SEALs receive at BUD/S trains recruits' brains to minimize the brain signal delay by generating fast, accurate reactions to situations. However despite all the advances in the training programs for SEALs, there are still a few "primal fears" that are much more difficult to overcome.

BUD/S students are taught seven techniques to help them overcome fear responses when dealing with overwhelming situations so that they will be able to remain in control of their actions and maintain their focus on achieving their objective.

They now know that they must use their minds to anticipate and identify any situation that will trigger one or more of the body's physical responses to fear or stress and to counter these responses very early, which allows them to remain calm and effective on the battlefield.

Because the SEALs have always engaged in very challenging and realistic training, it was very easy for them to incorporate the concept of "controlling fear" into it. SEALs (as are members of all SOF units) are constantly exposed to training that replicates the tempo, stress, as well as the physical and mental demands of actual combat situations. This exposure provides them with almost unlimited opportunities to practice utilizing these techniques to control their body's response to fear or threat stress.

By now, these seven fear suppressing techniques are so well known and have proven so effective that they have become part of the individual SEAL's "tool box," according to one Navy psychologist that was involved in the process of integrating them into SEAL training and development programs.

Seven Fear Suppressing Techniques

1. Segmenting Goals

This method was developed by psychologists who learned that some of the men failed BUD/S because they became overwhelmed at the thought of the amount of time they had yet to go as well as the tests and events they had yet to take. Their negative thoughts resulted in poor performance that led to their dismissal from the course, or they simply quit and gave up on their dream.

Opposite this mentality, the researchers found that those men who successfully graduated from the program, had opted to think about the training in short segments and focused on achieving one segment at a time throughout their time at BUD/S.

The prospect of the long months of training still yet to come and the many graded evolutions ahead was infinitely less daunting for those trainees who decided to break down the course into months, weeks, and then each day into each single task; then focused only on one segment or specific task at a time throughout each day.

2. Emotional Arousal Control

Arousal is the result of the chemical reaction that occurs during threat situations. Although this is a perfectly normal human reaction, it is detrimental to cognitive as well as motor effectiveness.

For a Navy SEAL the inability to be in control of their emotions, or to lose the ability to function at top levels could be fatal. SEALs and other special operators have used various forms of arousal control, among the most effective ones are deep breathing techniques, which help them regulate their heartbeat, allowing them to remain calm and focused on their mission.

A technique that is often referred to as "4 x 4 breathing" is an effective way to suppress the physiological effects of fear. Simply stated, the 4 x 4 breathing technique is executed by inhaling deeply, as though filling up your lungs, for four seconds, and then exhaling in a steady and even manner for four seconds. This sequence must be continuously repeated for two minutes or longer to be effective. I have utilized this technique countless times and know firsthand that it really works.

The reason why this technique works is because it basically tricks the brain into a state of calmness, which is associated with the most beneficial form of rest and recuperation derived from the rapid eye movement (REM) phase of the sleep pattern.

According to a medical doctor who works in the Naval Special Warfare community, this breathing technique is used by students as they prepare for daily training evolutions that are heavily weighted. This technique is not limited only to the time spent at selection courses; SEALs I have conversed with confirm that they continue to use this relaxation method long after they have graduated from BUD/S and gone on to serve in operational units.

Special operators from various SOF units have confirmed that breathing techniques are a widely used tool that helps control the fear response and allows them to remain calm and focused during dangerous situations. Learning how to use this technique effectively would be a definite asset if you are planning on attending a selection course, but it will also benefit you in any endeavor your undertake.

If you conduct a search on the internet, you will find that there are many variations of the breathing technique. The

"Bellows Breath," the "4-7-8 breathing exercise," "Breath Counting," "Box Breathing," to name a few. These are all effective, simple techniques that are easy to learn and master. Given the fact that controlling one's rate of breathing is a tried and true method for staving off some of the undesirable effects of arousal and the human stress response, it would be an important component that can be used for suppressing the effects of fear.

3. Visualization

The SEAL community has embraced visualization as an effective technique for combating the effects of fear during operations. It allows operators the ability to predict or anticipate various scenarios that could take place and how they can react to unplanned events or changes. Visualization doesn't just entail rehearsing what they might see, it is also necessary to include the feelings associated with each situation or scenario, as well as engaging the olfactory system to anticipate what they might smell during a threat situation or difficult challenge.

In this way, when an operator actually faces the situation, though it may be the first time he is physically engaged in it, in his mind he has already gone over it numerous times. This state of readiness in his mind serves to preempt the stress responses that would arise otherwise.

As previously mentioned, however, there are some *primal* fears that scientists believe are preprogrammed into our brains. One of these fears is the fear of drowning. For students going through the BUD/S course this fear is unavoidable. One of the most challenging exercises they must complete is the underwater pool competency test.

It requires students to remain under water for up to 20 minutes and take corrective action to resolve equipment problems with their SCUBA gear. During the exercise the instructors will sabotage the students by attacking them and snatching the regulators from their mouths, closing the tank air valves, disconnect or tie in knots the hoses from the tank. Because most students are not yet very comfortable underwater or using SCUBA gear, this is considered to be one of the most mentally challenging tests during the training program.

A student's performance can be deemed a failure if he panics and surfaces prematurely, if he takes too long to correct the equipment problems, if he is hesitant and appears too panicked, or if he lacks confidence under water. The students are given 4 attempts at this exercise, but will be recycled to a new class or dropped from the program if they fail to complete it.

Navy psychologists found that a majority of the successful students had experienced a significant degree of anxiety and apprehension for this training evolution given its difficulty. However, they also found that almost all of the students that successfully completed this evolution on the first attempt had utilized visualization as a technique to prepare for this event.

They visualized all the scenarios that could be thrown at them and knew the proper procedure for handling each problem they could face. They had practiced each maneuver several times and had gone over them in their minds over and over; as a result they were able to remain calm and focus solely on solving each problem rather than panicking during the test.

People in various professions that entail taking risks and involve high levels of stress have been using visualization techniques for a long time. If you have competed in sports at any level, more than likely you have utilized this technique at some point. Using this technique not only provides your mind the opportunity to engage in a series of rehearsals, it also sharpens your focus and helps you avoid distractions when you are working toward reaching a specific goal. I urge you to adopt and incorporate this technique and practice it as much as possible!

4. Positive Focus Within

Because most human beings think on average 500-1500 words per minute, it is important to make the nature of these internal "conversations" positive rather than negative. This technique is utilized by Navy SEALs to develop confidence and to maintain a high level of motivation.

If the focus of the thoughts is negative and contains words like "I can't" or "I'm going to fail," more than likely your performance will show them to be true. The positive focus or self-talk technique aims to replace negative thoughts with positive ones. If you tell yourself that "you're ready," or that "you can do this," then your performance will reflect those beliefs.

As students go through BUD/S, or Navy SEALs face tough situations in operations, positive self-talk can be a tremendous asset that will ensure success. When you face a difficult challenge it is important that you face it with a confident mindset believing that you will gain victory. You have to remind yourself that you CAN succeed, that you WILL NOT fail regardless of whatever pain you are feeling or what odds are against you.

Positive self-talk is perhaps the single most valuable tool that you can use to develop the mindset, confidence and resilience needed to achieve your goals.

5. Emotional Separation

It is a realistic expectation that most SEALs will witness or experience the loss of a friend during combat operations. For any of us this would be a difficult thing to go through. We would want to have the time to grief and go through the array of emotions that this type of loss would entail. Unfortunately SEALs don't have that luxury during a battle. They must find a way to put emotion aside and go on with their mission. Essentially, these men are taught to temporarily suspend their natural reactions to fear and the death and destruction that surrounds them. They learn to suppress normal human responses to extreme stress during the actual fight, knowing that they'll be able to address their emotions, the loss of friends, and other trauma at a later time, when it is safe to do so.

Although you probably won't encounter this type of traumatic loss, you may experience different kinds of setbacks at school or work. In order to be able to cope and keep focus on accomplishing your goals, it is important that you learn the technique of compartmentalization.

This concept will certainly be helpful if you decide to take on the challenge of becoming a Navy SEAL. It is almost a foregone conclusion that you will experience several setbacks, failures, and negative situations. It is essential that you be able to set them aside and focus on what lies ahead.

6. Plan for The Unexpected

Similar to visualization, contingency planning is an important technique that will help decrease the effects of fear and stress.

When time allows, operators will break down an entire operation from start to finish. They will design the plan, discuss various scenarios, and decide what alternate actions they will need to carry out depending on how a mission develops.

The main benefit of doing contingency planning is that the operators are acknowledging up front that the plan will probably not be executed flawlessly. This awareness will allow them to individually and collectively prepare for what may happen at various stages of the operation. As a result, they are typically able to adjust the battle plan, with little or no hesitation, during critical phases of an operation when lives are at stake and momentum must be maintained.

When you implement the contingency planning technique and face a task already knowing that things can change and that you are prepared for those changes will boost your confidence considerably. This confidence also enables rapid reaction to an obstacle or setback, which in turn enables you to avoid your body's normal response to stressors. Simply put, it's not about what happens during an important event or graded evolution, it's what you do in response to what happens that counts.

During BUD/S, a huge part of the instructors' job is to assess a candidate's reactions to situations as well as their decision-making abilities. In order to evaluate them on this element, they purposely place them in situations that will cause their plans to fail and leave them to figure out how to deal with it while they observe. Engaging in contingency planning is a superb way to enhance your chances of success, not only during selection, but in all aspects of your life!

7. Concentration and Focus

Because of the nature of their work, it is imperative for Navy SEALs to sharpen their focus to such a degree that when they are "in the zone" nothing—no distraction—could possibly penetrate or disrupt their concentration.

Although this degree of ultra-focus is necessary mostly while carrying out a training exercise or an actual mission, it is important that you learn now how to switch gears on a dime in order to go from relaxed mode to surgical sharpness without missing a beat. With time and practice you will be able to develop various routines that will help you reach this intense level or focus and concentration.

Adopt These Techniques!

Armed with the knowledge of these natural responses to fear and stress, and of the various techniques used by Navy SEALs to overcome them, you can implement them to better prepare yourself to deal with challenges and difficult situations.

As mentioned previously, these physical responses never go away; they remain with us as long as we live. A special operator's ability to learn how to anticipate and control these predictable and ever-present responses is what enables him to keep a "cool head" in very dangerous situations and perform at optimal levels.

The seven fear suppressing techniques have been effective in increasing the number of candidates who make it through selection. Make use of the information presented in these chapters and develop your ability to cope with the natural human responses to stress and fear.

Pursuit of Excellence

Navy SEALs are known for their physical prowess, their courage in battle, their proficiency in tactics, and their ability to succeed despite impossible odds. This awe-striking reputation is the result of an unwavering mindset that doesn't allow even the concept of defeat to ever be considered.

Everywhere you go, you will find exceptional leaders who have risen to the top and set the example for all to follow. These are the people who are highly regarded and who set the standard in everything they do. Because of their work ethic, enthusiasm, and professionalism, they have earned the respect of everyone around them, even those who hold positions above theirs. Most of us dream of someday having that type of success—to be regarded as the best.

An instructor a BUD/S once welcomed his class by telling them that they had a decision to make. He explained that there was no reason why any of them should not be able to make it through the course and that it all came down to two choices: Choose to give in to self-doubt and fear, or choose to be exceptional and pursue the dream of becoming an elite warrior.

Navy SEALs possess one trait that sets them apart from most people: The *relentless pursuit of excellence* that SEALs demonstrate in all they do. This trait lies at the core of the spirit of the Navy SEAL community. They simply choose to pursue excellence in everything they do. It isn't easy to achieve, it doesn't just happen—it requires dedication and self-discipline.

One of my favorite quotes comes from Richard Machowicz's *Unleash the Warrior Within*. It is a testament of the mental fortitude that most SEALs display:

> *I had to get myself in the mindset of never giving up no matter what. A buddy of mine gave me a quote which stated, 'A man can only be beaten in two ways: if he gives up or he dies.' I had that quote in my wallet until the pencil marks rubbed off. I really lived that motto. I decided that if I am not dead, then I cannot quit.*

This simple quote gave Machowicz the motivation he needed to fulfill his dream of being one of the exceptional men he admired. No amount of pain, no suffering, nothing short of dying would deter him from his goal.

I wish I could tell you that there is a quick and easy way to achieve this level of excellence. The truth is that there are no short-cuts. It is ultimately up to you to do the work. It won't be easy and it won't be fast, it is a hard road that takes time, effort, and a lot of heart. Just being a good performer won't cut it. You have to give everything you have just to make it to the next day. Just like managing stress, you have to focus on one piece at a time. So don't worry about the test you have in the afternoon. Your goal is to make it to breakfast. Then lunch, and so on. If you wake up knowing that every day will pose new challenges and that you are ready to face them head-on, you will be well equipped to achieve any goal you set.

Everything you've read so far focuses on a simple concept that is the foundation of SEAL success: Pursue excellence in everything you do, execute all tasks with vigor and intensity; *winning* can be the only acceptable outcome.

It's your decision to make. Think about what goals you are striving to achieve. Whatever your objective may be, chances are it will require some level of focus, self-discipline, and determination. It's as simple as that, no more excuses, simply go "all in" and *decide* that you are going to become an exceptional person.

Becoming Mentally Tough

As stated previously, the definition of mental toughness is difficult to pin-point, but we have presented various traits that are present in anyone who is considered to be mentally tough. So this leads me to believe that mental toughness can in fact be taught.

It is also my belief that developing mental toughness should not be limited to only those who are preparing to become Navy SEALs, but rather it should be undertaken by everyone who has a goal to achieve. It doesn't matter what your goal or objective is, mental toughness is essential to its achievement.

What Does Mental Toughness Look Like for You

Depending on what your desired outcome or final objective is, you should define what mental toughness looks like for you. If you are contemplating joining the Navy SEALs or other branch of the special operations community, you will inevitably need to be mentally and physically fit in order to meet the demands of training and operations down the line. You will need to be able to withstand unimaginable amounts of pain, remain motivated despite the difficult challenges you're facing, and be willing to put your life at risk every day.

However if your goal is something other than that, you will still need mental toughness to be able to achieve it. Your definition of mental toughness might be:

- Running a race you don't think you can finish.
- Starting your own business.
- Learning a new skill.
- Changing your eating habits.
- Being promoted at work.
- Writing your first book.

Once you have a clear picture of what you want to accomplish you can begin to formulate a plan for how you can achieve it. It will be easier to develop the mental toughness necessary by associating your goals with actionable tasks that you can track. The main thing to understand is that mental toughness requires action, you can't wait for it to simply happen for you, you actually have to take steps to make it happen.

Find Comfort in Discomfort

Whatever challenge you set for yourself, ultimately your success will depend upon your ability to persevere and push through situations or periods of time that bring forth various forms of discomfort, anxiety, and self-doubt. Accepting that every day will bring forth new problems to solve, turmoil, and even setbacks and failure, will help you build your confidence and will increase your mental toughness every day. The time will come when you might even actually look forward to it!

Elevating your Level of Mental Toughness

I would like to introduce you to some basic ways in which you can begin increasing your mental toughness.

1. Begin

Yes, very simply, get started! All that this step will require is for you to **make the decision** that you are 100% committed to this goal. I know it sounds very simple, and it really is simple, but it's not *easy*. This time, though, I think that by following these tips it will be much easier to reach your goal. This step is crucial though. You must commit. There's a switch that goes off in your mind when you truly commit to something—this is the beginning phase of gaining mental toughness.

2. Milestones

Most challenging goals will take time to achieve. Sometimes thinking about how long something is going to take to finish, stops you from even starting it. Don't focus on how to get the whole thing done, just break it down into smaller goals and check them off as you go.

It is better to set attainable goals that you can work toward and focus on rather than having a huge unattainable dream looming over you. If, for example, your dream is to be able to run a marathon, and all you can think about is how in the world you are going to make it through 26.2 miles, you might never even sign up for the race. But when you break down your training into increments over a period of time, then at the beginning of the training you only need to focus on running 3 miles.

Once you start accomplishing these small goals your confidence will start to grow and you will start to feel a new sense of purpose. You will begin to believe that this huge dream that seemed unattainable, might just be possible.

3. Don't Let Setbacks Set You Back

You may be doing everything right, you have your plan, you've set your goals, you are achieving and progressing, and then there's an unexpected change. Whether is a deadline being moved on you, or the location of a performance or game, or maybe you get sick or injured. You can't let any of these setbacks derail you. Simply look at the situation and adjust your plan accordingly.

There's a well know saying in the armed forces: "Not even the best plan survives the first shot." This means that it doesn't matter how sound a battle plan may be, the moment the shooting starts there will be chaos and things will go wrong, and the plan will need to be adjusted.

This is good advice for anyone in any situation. When an obstacle suddenly arises that threatens to derail your plan, simply acknowledge and accept that there's a setback, adapt and adjust calmly, and KEEP GOING!

4. Become an Early Riser

When you wake up early and start your day achieving *something*, over time the cumulative effects of that extra hour or two of dedicated daily effort will yield significant results. One former special operator who is now a highly-successful entrepreneur told me that getting up earlier and attacking his task list while almost everyone else (including his competition) is still sleeping is his "secret weapon." He, like many other early-risers, feels that he often accomplishes more before 8am than he does during the rest of the day.

Initially, it may be difficult to think about changing your sleeping habits, but the human body is very adaptable, and after approximately two weeks you will find that you will have adjusted to the change and it will become part of your routine. Just as discussed above, don't look at it as this huge lifestyle change, simply try it out for a week, then two weeks, and so on. Making this change successfully will also further develop your mental toughness.

5. Get outside Your Comfort Zone

You cannot develop mental toughness unless you attempt things that challenge you in a significant way. The more you try new, scary things, the broader that comfort zone will become.

I can say without reservation that almost all of the special operators I have had the pleasure of working with demonstrated a great amount of eagerness to try and learn new things in their professional and personal lives. They figured out that your levels of mental and physical capacity either grow or decrease—depending on how much you are exercising them—but they don't remain constant without some type of challenge.

Don't become stagnant, always strive to advance your knowledge, increase your physical ability, and expand your horizons. Try different foods, go to new places, learn a new language, start a new hobby, these are all various ways in which you can take yourself out of your comfort zone and develop your mental toughness.

6. Control your Fears

It is critical for Navy SEALs to be able to remain focused even when the threat of injury or death is near. In order to function under these conditions, Navy SEALs go through intense, extensive training to learn how to anticipate those situations, implement the steps to override the natural human response, and neutralize its effect on their performance.

Even if your goal isn't to become a SEAL, these techniques will help you in achieving any objective you have set your sights on. These techniques will give you the tools to overcome challenges, maintain focus, and carry on until you reach your goal.

7. Find a Mentor

I'm sure that throughout your life you have met people whom you admire and wish to emulate. People who have worked hard, faced the odds, and come out victorious in the end. You have probably watched them put forth a tremendous effort, never wavering, never giving in to despair, but always steadily working toward their goals.

If you are fortunate enough to know someone like that, you should definitely put in the effort to strike up conversations with them and work on building a relationship of trust and respect. Mentorship will undoubtedly follow.

8. The Power of Knowledge

One of the easiest ways to gain knowledge is through reading. When you find a topic that interests you, with today's technology, it won't be difficult to find countless articles and material on the subject. Take a look at anyone who is the best in their field and you will probably find that they are always well versed on the latest and greatest information available in their field. This is because they are constantly reading and studying any new discoveries or material related to their field.

A common misconception about Navy SEALs is that they are big muscular guys with a lot of guts but not a lot of brains. This couldn't be farther from the truth. Navy SEALs are required to expertly know and understand countless facts about geography, cartography, tactics, languages, customs and traditions of various places, weapons systems, technology, and a myriad other topics.

In this day in age, there truly is no excuse for the average person not to be able to acquire knowledge on any topic that is of interest to them. Remember knowledge is power, and in difficult situations, having an edge can help you overcome many obstacles.

9. Shared Interests

As you journey toward accomplishing your goal, whatever it may be, make sure to reach out and find others who share the same interests. The knowledge you can gain from simple conversations with others who share your same goals is priceless. They will also understand better than most what you may be feeling as you travel the same path. They will become part of your support network.

Developing mental toughness should be at the top of your to-do list regardless of what goals you have set for yourself. It is fair to say that if you are going to be in a field where physical strength and prowess are a requirement, then mental toughness will play a significant role in your success. But keep in mind that mental toughness is essential to success even in professions where very little physical exertion occurs.

You now know that mental toughness can in fact be learned, developed, and optimized. You have the knowledge, you have the tools, and all you have to do is put it into practice!

The Meaning of Success

For each of us, success has a distinct meaning. We each define it differently depending on our goals in life. There are many variables that will impact that definition. The stage of our lives we are living, experiences we've had, and the advantages or disadvantages we have lived with.

It is important to express in some way what your vision of success looks like. You can write it down, or draw a picture and make sure that it is visible every day. It is also critical that you define some short term and long term goals that go along with it. It is important for you to see how you are progressing on the path to achieving your notion of success.

It's ok for that definition to change over the course of the years. As you go through life many factors will change that will influence your decisions, and by default, may alter your vision of the future. But it is important that you never lose sight of the goals you want to accomplish.

Remember to stay positive no matter what challenges you face. The key to success lies in your diligence, preparation, and constant pursuit of excellence. Become mentally tough, be knowledgeable in your field, and most importantly never, ever give up! Success is within your reach, you just have to decide to go for it!

Made in the USA
San Bernardino, CA
28 February 2018